GIFT WRAPPINGS

FOR EVERY OCCASION

Personalize your
gifts with a wealth of
inspirational ideas

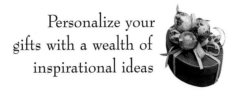

GILL DICKINSON

GIFT WRAPPINGS

FOR EVERY OCCASION

Personalize your
gifts with a wealth of
inspirational ideas

CHARTWELL
BOOKS, INC.

A QUINTET BOOK

Published by Chartwell Books
A Division of Book Sales, Inc.
114 Northfield Avenue
Edison N.J. 08837

This edition produced for sale
in the U.S.A., its territories
and dependencies only.

ISBN 0-7858-0155-3

This book was designed and produced by
Quintet Publishing Limited
6 Blundell Street
London N7 9BH

Creative Director: Richard Dewing
Designer: Ian Hunt
Project Editor: Katie Preston
Illustrator: Katie Sleight
All Photography by Paul Forrester
Except: pages 52, 53, 57, 58 & 59, by Tim Hill

Typeset in Great Britain by Ian Hunt Design, Brighton
Manufactured in Hong Kong by Regent Publishing Services Limited
Printed in China by Leefung-Asco Printers Limited

ACKNOWLEDGMENT
Herbs and spices supplied by Schwartz

CONTENTS

INTRODUCTION

There seem to be more and more occasions for exchanging gifts ...
Christmas, birthdays, Easter, Hallowe'en, weddings, Saint Valentine's
Day, Mother's Day ... the list goes on. How many times have you
complained about the price of your store bought wrapping paper while
hunting for your scissors and cellophane tape? How many times have
you felt disappointed when the wrapping on that expensive gift looks
uninspired and just plain untidy? Now you can learn how to make your
gift wrapping as beautiful and original as your gifts.

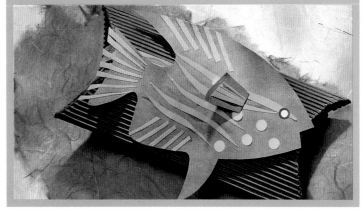

Homemade, decorated
boxes and envelopes make
delightful, original
wrapping paper.

Crepe paper and paper
fans are a simple way
of giving an Oriental
flavor to your gift
wrapping paper.

Give a new lease of life to old shopping bags and boxes by gluing on plain or painted string patterns.

BE ORIGINAL

In the pages that follow you will find a wealth of inspirational ideas and techniques for creating dozens of different looks for your gifts. Whether you need to wrap a gift for a dedicated gardener – cover the wrapping paper with dried leaves and berries – or a fun gift for a child – make a giant pencil and fill it with novelty pens, pencils, and crayons – there is an original idea to delight everyone.

NATURALLY BEAUTIFUL

The emphasis throughout is on using natural and recycled materials to create beautiful homemade gift-wrap. There is no need to buy expensive ribbons, wrapping paper, and gift tags when you can find an amazing range of materials and inspiration all around you: in your backyard, on the beach, or among the things you might otherwise throw away.

KEEP COLLECTING

Keep a box for your collection of gift wrapping accessories, from old buttons to odds and ends of ribbon and string. Whenever you take a walk along a beach or in a forest, keep an eye out for interesting natural objects such as shells, driftwood, seaweed, leaves, pine cones, berries, and flowers. You will need to dry out leaves and flowers before using them – simply place them between layers of paper and weight them down for a couple of weeks.

FAMILY FUN

Most of the projects and techniques can be enjoyed by the whole family. Kids will love making their own wrapping paper and tags with potato printing, paint spattering, and simple stencils. If you use recycled materials, by decorating plain brown paper for example, these techniques are also inexpensive. If you run out of ideas, you can always rely on your kids to think up something original!

A selection of decorated papers. The techniques used include stenciling and spattering.

PAPER, BOXES AND CONTAINERS

• Reuse paper whenever possible – tissue paper, brown paper, and even old wrapping paper will come in useful. Spatter paint onto crumpled tissue paper for instant, original wrapping paper.

• Buy recycled or rough paper from a store selling artists' materials – these come in wonderful colors and are also inexpensive.

• Keep an eye out for recycled metallic paper and cellophane – they have a softer, more natural look than nonrecycled ones.

• Hold onto any boxes and containers you are given. Chocolates and cookies often come in fancy packaging that can be repainted and decorated.

• Put awkward-shaped presents in boxes before wrapping them – it makes it much easier to make the gift look good!

• Glass jars, even ordinary jelly jars, are great for filling with homemade candy and truffles. Decorate with ribbons or paper cutouts.

• Paint old pieces of corrugated paper and wrap them around candles or bottles.

• Make small sacks and bags from different materials, from muslin to hessian, for simple gift-wrapping.

• Use envelopes and folders as another way to wrap presents. Two templates are given – one for a simple, flat envelope and one for the three-dimensional (3-D) envelope used on page 23. Clear folders make fun gifts when filled with pretty stationery and pens.

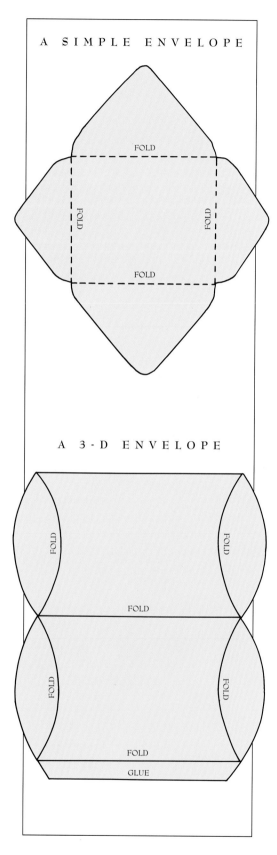

A SIMPLE ENVELOPE

FOLD

FOLD

FOLD

FOLD

A 3-D ENVELOPE

FOLD

FOLD

FOLD

FOLD

FOLD

FOLD

GLUE

STRING, RIBBON, AND WIRE

• Before buying expensive ribbons, have a look in your shed or tool-box – garden twine, raffia, string, and wire are all inexpensive and have great textures.

• Paper ribbon comes in wonderful colors and, when unraveled, makes very impressive bows.

• As an alternative to silky ribbons, try paper and cotton braid.

• Paint on some extra decorations or pierce a pattern in paper braid.

• You will need some different thicknesses of florist's wire when working with dried flowers and berries.

PAINT, SCISSORS, AND GLUE

• Try to form a collection of different paints in a range of colors. For most jobs poster colors will work well. Gouache is useful for finer details – when decorating eggs or for fine stencils. Oil paints are useful for the marbling paper technique.

• You will also need a range of paintbrushes, including stenciling brushes. Keep an old toothbrush for paint spattering. Household paintbrushes are good for covering large areas quickly.

• Use masking fluid – don't give it to young children – to create interesting "resist" effects on paper, cardboard, and even eggs!

• Use scissors where possible. If necessary, use a craft knife, but take care and always use a cutting mat. Pinking shears are useful for instant and interesting paper effects.

• You will need some white, all-purpose craft glue capable of sticking paper, cardboard, fabric, plastic, and string. This takes about an hour to dry, so some quick-drying clear adhesive will also be useful.

• Avoid spray adhesives. These are not very effective for anything other than paper, and are not very safe or environmentally friendly.

• You will also need masking tape, double-sided cellophane tape and ordinary cellophane tape.

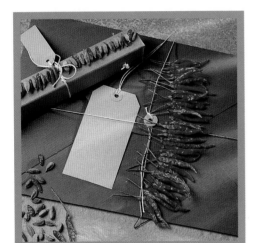

These gifts have a fresh, natural look. The packages were tied with string, and the chilies were threaded onto florist's wire.

WRAPPING A BOX

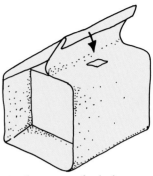

1 Cut the paper to fit the box. You will need an overlap at the top of about 4 inches and two thirds the box height at the sides. Fold down the top by 3/4 inch from the edge. Center the fold on the box and hold down with double-sided cellophane tape.

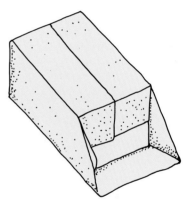

2 Center the box in the paper and press the folded edge against the box. Crease the side folds before pushing them in.

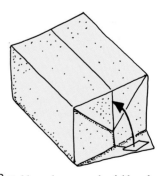

3 Fold up the triangular fold and secure with double-sided cellophane tape. Repeat at the other end of the box.

CHAPTER ONE

BACK TO NATURE

Seeds, pods, spices, and fruit dry easily and quickly. They make fragrant and beautiful additions to your gifts as well as great Christmas tree decorations. Prepare fruit and spices in the Fall so you have a wealth of material ready for the festive season. A single layer of citrus slices and spices kept in a warm, dry place will be ready to use in three to four weeks. Fresh and dried herbs and spices can be bought from supermarkets and specialist food stores. Coordinate this natural look by using green and brown boxes, raffia, and string.

1 Thread slices of citrus fruits, bay leaves and bunches of cinnamon sticks onto a length of raffia. Tie on some heart-shaped cookies. Attach this gorgeous garland to your wrapped box.

2 Tie natural raffia around a box and decorate with a heart-shaped cookie.

3 Tie a box with ribbon and green raffia and decorate with sliced oranges and lemons.

FRUIT AND SPICE

A selection of dried fruit, seed, and spice decorations. The method for making the spice balls is shown on page 15. Make some hearts from florist's wire and thread on dried cranberries and cardamoms.

Tie some dried oranges, raffia, and berries into a bunch and attach to a natural straw heart. You can hang this from a mantelpiece or door or simply tie it onto a gift.

HOT AND SPICY

You can buy chilies ready-dried or dry them yourself. Red chilies look great on gold boxes and bags. Thread together some small chilies for a small gift. Use a couple of large chilies on a bigger present.

Decorate a large envelope with a garland of dried chilies and a brown label. Thread tiny chilies and cardamoms alternately onto string and tie onto a box.

Spice Balls

These beautiful, fragrant spice balls make a colorful
and exotic addition to any gift. Fill a plain brown box
with a selection of cooking spices or potpourri, tie
with natural-colored raffia, and attach a spice ball.

1 Push a length of
wire into a styrofoam ball
and fold in one end of the
wire to make a small loop.
Draw a spiral of glue
around the ball. Carefully
stick on the sunflower
seeds.

2 When this glue has
dried, draw a second
spiral of glue onto the
ball. Decorate with dried
corn kernels. Leave the
ball to dry completely.

3 Thread some raffia
through the loop on the
base of the ball. Repeat
at the top, leaving enough
raffia to hang the
ball. Glue on some dried
bay leaves.

Gingerbread

Make some gift bags extra special by using some homemade gingerbread. Use dried cranberries, bay leaves, and chilies for extra decoration. This is a fun project for the family to try out together.

INGREDIENTS

$1/3$ cup granulated brown sugar

2 tbsp corn syrup

1 tbsp molasses

2 tbsp water

$1/2$ cup butter

$1/2$ tsp baking soda

1 cup plain flour

1 tsp ground ginger

1 tsp cinnamon

1 Bring the sugar, syrup, molasses, and water to a boil, stirring well.

2 Remove the pan from the heat and add the butter and baking soda. Stir in the flour and spices and mix well.

3 Leave the dough for 1 hour. Preheat the oven to 350°F. Roll out the dough on a floured board until it is $1/8$ inch thick. Cut out the gingerbread shapes and place on a buttered cookie sheet.

4 Bake the gingerbread for 10 – 12 minutes. Pierce holes for hanging while the cookies are still warm. Cool on a wire tray.

1 Decorate a red bag with a paper ribbon bow, raffia, and decorated gingerbread.

2 Decorate a blue bag with threaded chilies and cinnamon sticks.

3 Decorate gingerbread with cranberries and bay leaves, and tie onto a bag.

4 Thread cranberries onto a wire heart, and tie onto some gingerbread with raffia.

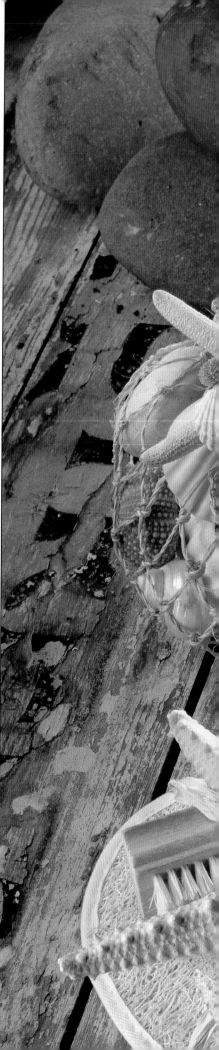

CHAPTER TWO

BESIDE THE SEASIDE

 A walk along the seashore will produce a wealth of both inspiration and materials for your gift wrapping. The textures and colors of natural objects such as shells, pebbles, stones, seaweed, and driftwood make beautiful additions to gifts and help you to achieve unique results with very little effort. Alternatively, decorate your gifts with shapes from the undersea world – fish and sea horses for example – the choice is limited only by your imagination.

1 Make a simple drawstring bag in natural fabric and cover with stones. Finish with a shell label.

2 Fill a large shell with gifts for the bathroom, tie with raffia and add a tag.

3 Fill a string bag with shells and natural sponges. Decorate with a starfish.

4 Wrap a small bar of soap in natural-colored paper and tie with raffia. Decorate with stones.

5 A round luffa makes a good base for a gift; finish up with raffia and a starfish.

PAPERS

These delicate tissue papers have been decorated with relief fabric paint. The paints are very easy to draw with and can be used straight from the tube. Create a simple seashore pattern, seaweed and shells for example, and add some small pieces of torn tissue for extra decoration.

TAGS

The gold-and-white tags and wooden fish were sold as
decorations for Christmas trees, but they make
stunning additions to gifts. Simple fish and shell
shapes can be cut out from paper and decorated with
spattered paint or strips of tissue paper. A few
templates are given on page 106. You can also make
small cuts in the tags to give a little more texture.

DECORATING WITH SHELLS

1 Stitch together two pieces of white muslin to make a bag. Using clear adhesive, stick on small shells, fill the bag with bath salts, then tie the top with raffia.

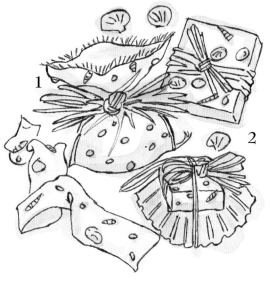

2 Wrap boxes and soaps with white muslin and again decorate with shells and raffia. Place small gifts on a large flat shell to make a bigger impact.

BENEATH THE WAVES

These simple boxes were made from corrugated paper.
You can find the pattern for this type of box on page 8.
Decorate the boxes with paper fish (template on page
106). Decorated boxes are an ideal way to present
difficult shapes such as neckties and scarves.

Torn Paper

Overlapping layers of torn paper give an interesting, textured look to a gift. You can use either bought paper or decorate your own. Tissue paper is ideal since it comes in a wonderful range of colors, it is translucent, and is inexpensive.

1 Cover a box with tissue and decorate with torn paper, raffia, and shells.

2 Wrap a box with turquoise torn paper. Decorate with pieces of raffia and a chocolate fish.

3 Use speckled paper to wrap a box, decorate with torn paper, raffia, and a starfish.

4 Decorate a box with silver netlike fabric, raffia, and novelty chocolate fish.

1 Wrap the box with blue tissue paper. Tear off two strips of light-blue textured paper and wrap around the gift, securing with cellophane tape.

2 Choose two colors of tissue paper. Tear off a mixture of small and large strips, then glue to the box.

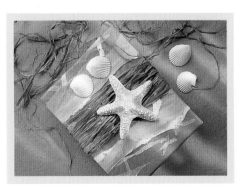

3 Wrap colored raffia around the middle of the box, tying it at the back with a knot. Decorate with shells.

 Collect shells whenever you go on vacation. When you travel to exotic locations, make sure you do not take away rare shells that may be protected by law.

Complement these naturally beautiful objects by using handmade and recycled papers to wrap your gifts. A beautiful handmade box is a wonderful gift in itself and can be filled with bath salts, soaps, or simply more shells.

1 Wrap a strip of paper ribbon around a textured paper shopping bag and decorate with grass and shells.

2 Use a small amount of clear adhesive to attach shells straight onto a small bag.

3 Thread shells or sea urchins onto a piece of raffia. Attach to the lid of a box.

4 Personalize some bought paper and envelopes by decorating with shells. Pierce a hole in the shell with a needle, then thread with raffia.

CHAPTER THREE
PERFECT PAPER

Paper is a very versatile medium. You can create wonderful three-dimensional and textured effects with simple techniques. Both children and adults will enjoy folding, cutting, creasing, curling, and pleating papers to create original and inexpensive wrapping paper. You will need some fine-to medium-strength paper in a range of colors, scissors or a craft knife, a cutting mat, and glue or cellophane tape.

1 Lightly fold plain paper around the box. Lay it flat again and mark out the circular pattern in pencil, on two sides of the box only. Cut out the pattern with a craft knife. Wrap the box and decorate with shredded paper.

2 A small gift can look effective by cutting a pattern in only part of the paper. Add a cut-paper tag.

3 A colored box showing through cut paper gives an interesting effect.

Cut Paper I

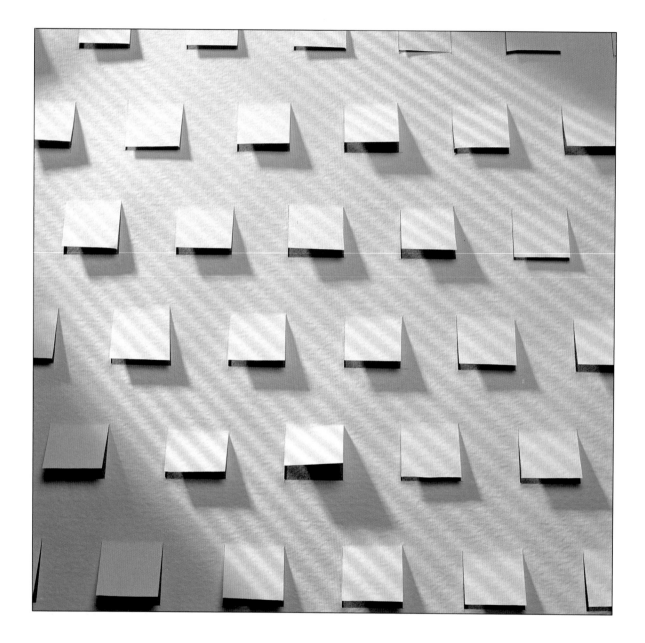

A simple cut-out pattern, like these regularly spaced squares, gives an interesting effect with little effort. You will need a cutting mat, craft knife, ruler, and pencil. Draw a simple grid making sure that, when you cut the squares, they do not run into one another.

CUT PAPER II

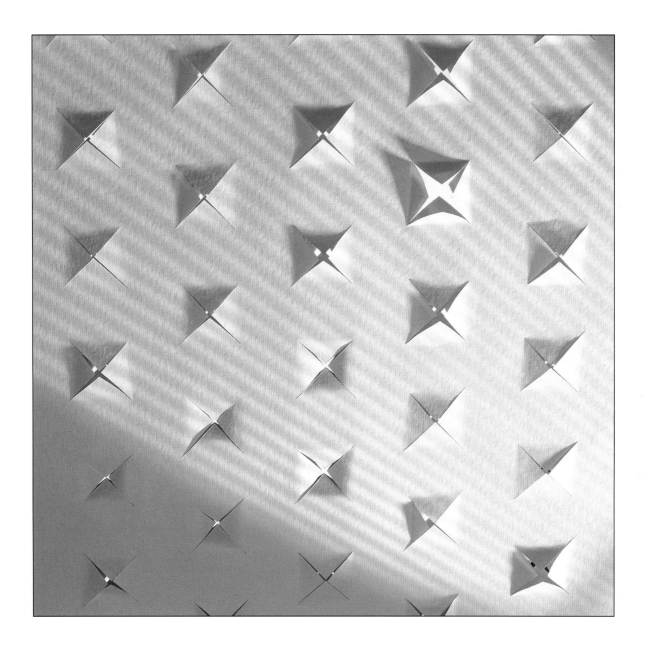

You can make a cut-paper pattern as complicated as you wish. Mark out another square grid, but this time cut the diagonals, rather than three sides of the square. Use a steel ruler and a craft knife or sharp scissors if possible.

FLOWER POWER

Make a card by folding some handmade or embossed paper in half. Cut out a vase from plain, white paper and cut two rows of small "v" shapes across the top. Glue the sides of the vase to the cardboard. Cut out some flower and leaf shapes, then glue or tape these inside the vase.

WHITE WEDDING

Use medium-strength paper for this larger-cutwork wrapping paper. Repeat the triangular pattern on the tag. The decorative bow is made by folding strips of paper and attaching them to the top of the box. Use a sharp craft knife to achieve clean, precise lines.

PRETTY IN PINK

Wrap presents in pretty pastel-colored paper and add strips of coordinating colors. Add extra interest by cutting the edges of the paper into zigzags and curves, or use pinking shears. Make some matching flowers as shown on page 36.

PLEASING PASTELS

Cut several leaves and flowers (see page 107) from thin paper. Pierce a hole in the center of the flowers and thread onto 1 inch of rolled-up paper. Glue onto the gift with some paper leaves.

Make some simple coordinating tags for these gifts. You will need some matching papers, all of similar thickness, scissors, pinking shears, a hole punch, and glue. Make some small flowers for extra decoration.

Paper Flowers

A simple gift of stationery can be made extra special by wrapping decorative strips of colored paper around the center. Add a pencil or pen decorated to look like a flower, and a leaf tag.

1 Cut several strips of colored paper and cut patterns along the edges. Wrap these around the gift. Wrap a pencil or pen in green paper.

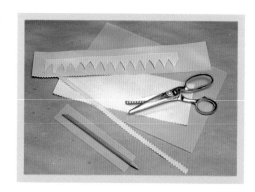

2 Cut out several petal shapes in paper, then curl over the ends. Cut a 2 inch strip of paper and make cuts in it (templates on page 107). Wrap around the pencil and then glue on the petals one by one.

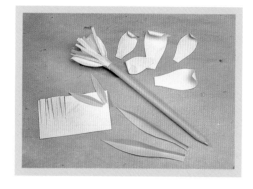

3 Cut out some leaf shapes and glue onto the pencil. Cut a leaf for the tag, make a hole, and thread through a thin strip of paper (to attach leaf tag to the gift).

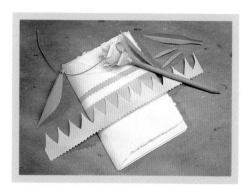

A homemade cracker makes a very special gift. The method is shown on page 66. Choose the materials and colors to reflect the occasion – in this case paper in white and pastel colors. The traditional wedding almonds are tied in white net and placed on decorated crepe paper.

Keep a collection of boxes and containers for your gift wrapping. Cover a box in thin paper and decorate with cut-out shapes and paper flowers.

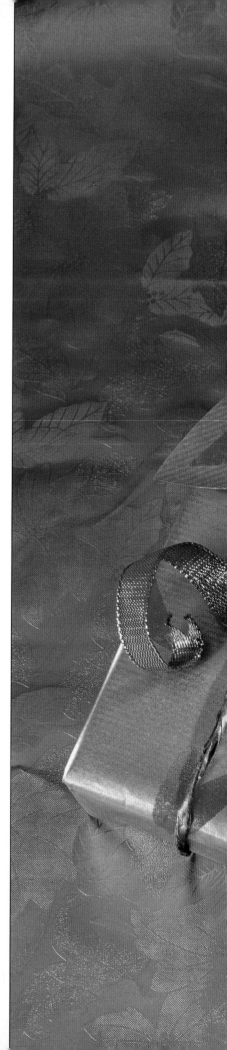

CHAPTER FOUR

GIFTS FROM THE HEART

The heart is a symbol of love and friendship. Heart images can be used on gifts for many different occasions – for Mother's Day, a wedding, a baptism and, of course, for Saint Valentine's Day. Hearts can be very decorative or simple, symmetrical, or more stylized. The inspirational ideas that follow range from a simple heart-shaped box with a handmade tag to wire hearts threaded with flowers. Look for old heart-shaped boxes and containers that can be repainted or decorated.

1 Stencil red hearts onto gold paper and use matching gold paper ribbon and tag.

2 Stencil gold hearts onto a red heart-shaped box. Add a bow made of fine strands of ribbon and a tag with beads on it.

3 Tie a round box with two different thicknesses of ribbon. Add a wooden tag that has been decorated with fabric relief paint.

Papers

These three papers were made using a very simple
piercing technique, described on page 48. Designs can
be repetitive or random, and the sizes of the holes can
be varied to emphasize different parts of the design.
Any simple shape or pattern works well.

SUGAR HEARTS

Instead of buying a box of chocolates, make or buy some heart-shaped truffles. Place them on a heart-shaped plate and wrap with cellophane. Decorate with transparent ribbon and a heart tag. Make a card from recycled paper, glue gauze ribbon down the front, then tie on a paper heart with raffia. The wooden heart has been decorated with dried flowers and raffia and can be tied onto a gift.

Dried flowers are a very simple way to decorate a gift. This can also be very economical if you have a well-stocked garden. Most florists have a large selection of dried flowers, and they can advise on which fresh flowers dry well – roses, hydrangeas, lavender, bay leaves, and sunflowers are just a few examples. Look out for unusual boxes and baskets made in natural materials such as cane and willow. Flowers not only make wonderful, long-lasting gifts, but they also smell delicious.

1 Fill a hollow wooden heart with lavender and decorate with dried sunflower heads.

2 Place some painted-heart boxes on top of each other and secure with paper ribbon. Decorate with sprigs of lavender, roses, and bay leaves.

3 Tie together small bunches of lavender with wire and cut the stems 1½ inch from the flowers. Tie the bunches around the edge of a heart-shaped basket with pieces of wire. Be sure to fill in all the gaps.

HEARTS AND FLOWERS

These delicate miniature wreaths make beautiful
presents in themselves, but can also be added to other
gifts. Make a simple heart shape from florist's wire
and decorate with any flowers you have at hand.
Pierce rosebuds with a needle, and thread onto the
wire. Glue rose petals onto a wire heart and decorate
the top with flowers. For a large heart, make small
bunches of grasses, flowers, and leaves and tie onto
the heart with more wire.

HEARTFELT GIFTS

Carefully coordinate all the elements of your gifts – wrapping paper, ribbon, tag, and cardboard. Make each gift more special by adding your own decoration to the elements bought from a store.

1 Wrap individual soaps with recycled paper. Tie with cotton ribbon decorated with fabric relief paint. Place the gifts in a wire soap dish and add a homemade lavender bag.

2 Make your own card with handmade paper. Cut one heart from corrugated paper and tear another from purple recycled paper. Thread a gold wire heart through the corrugated paper.

Pierced Paper

The technique of piercing paper can be used for wrapping paper, tags, ribbons, and cards. The delicate effect is achieved by piercing the paper with the fine point of a needle or nail. Although hearts have been used here, any simple design will be effective.

1 Take two pieces of colored paper and two sizes of heart stencil (see page 107). Cut out one of each size.

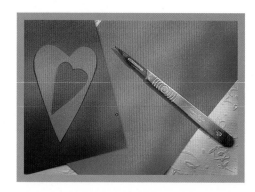

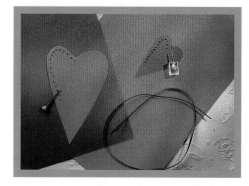

2 You will need two sizes of needle. Lay your hearts on a soft blanket. Pierce the edge of the larger heart with the thicker point.

3 Repeat the process with the smaller heart and needle. Pierce a hole through the top of both hearts and thread with a ribbon.

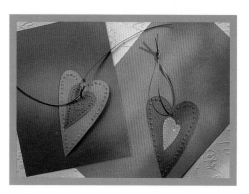

Wrap boxes in corrugated paper and decorate with pierced paper ribbon and tags. Glue some small hearts onto pieces of wire and gather into a bunch to decorate the gifts.

STRAIGHT TO THE HEART

Adorn some simple boxes (above) with a few little personal touches. Decorate ribbon with fabric relief paint and make your own tag; cut out one large heart outline and tie on a smaller, pierced paper heart with raffia.

Make some original paper by stenciling large white hearts onto some bought red paper. Make a matching red-and-white tag. Wrap a box (left) with the paper and tie with white paper ribbon. Decorate with a chocolate heart.

TAGS

The metal tags were originally designed to hang on Christmas trees, but will enhance any Saint Valentine's Day gift. The pierced paper tags range from simple designs to complicated patterns. The wooden tags have been decorated by gluing on a few heart sequins, stenciling on heart shapes, or adding a small bunch of dried flowers.

CHAPTER FIVE
AUTUMN LEAVES

Leaves are a wonderful form of natural decoration. They come in all shapes, sizes, and colors and, best of all, are completely free! Collect leaves all year round – on country walks, in the backyard or on your way to work or school – place them between layers of newspaper and weight them down with books for about two weeks. You will be left with a large selection of shapes to use for labels, paper, and decoration. When using leaf motifs, reflect the shades of fall, from soft greens, ocher and burnt sienna to browns and gold. Use raffia or string in natural colors.

1 Wrap boxes in paper spattered with autumnal-colored paints and tie with string. Make more of a small gift by placing it on a large cut-out leaf.

2 Wrap gifts with brown paper and tie with raffia or string. Spatter the whole present with gold paint and decorate with a metal leaf tag.

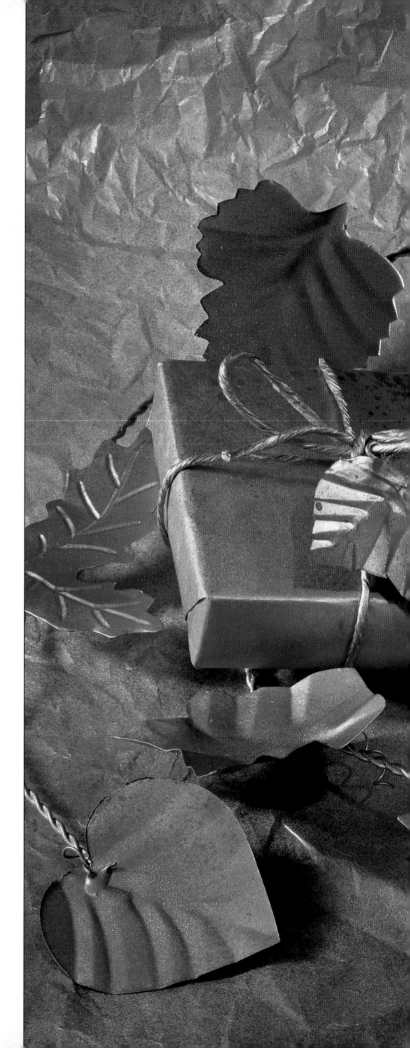

PAPERS

These spattered and stenciled papers have been made on a range of paper thicknesses and types. Medium-strength handmade papers can be used and look wonderful with natural forms stenciled onto them. Spattered papers are made by placing leaves at random on paper and securing them with double-sided tape. Spatter (see page 60) with a mixture of rich greens and lift off the leaves when dry. Use the leaves for labels or for extra decoration.

TAGS

A mixture of decorative leaf shapes. Real leaves can be used as templates for cutting shapes out of brown paper. Paint or spatter the paper leaves with gouache or poster color, or leave brown. Punch a hole in the tag and thread through string or raffia to tie to the gift.

Stenciling

The key to stenciling is to use a dry brush. This will give good results and helps the stencil to last. Tie your wrapped boxes with raffia. Any scraps of stenciled paper can be added to a plain gift to give a different look.

1 Choose an interesting leaf and draw around it onto medium-thickness paper. Leave a generous border for neat stenciling.

2 Cut out the leaf carefully. If you do not want to use a craft knife, copy one of the templates from pages 108 – 9 onto a piece of paper, fold in half, and cut out with scissors.

3 Mix the paint to a thick consistency and keep the brush dry. Lay the stencil over the paper and lightly dab the paint evenly. Use two colors for a richer effect.

 You can collect natural objects, such as leaves, pine cones, and berries, all year round. You should also keep an eye out for unusual gifts, particularly when traveling abroad. A bundle of these twig pencils with a spattered leaf tag makes a great, natural-style gift. Alternatively, just one pencil placed under the bow of a gift with the tag attached adds an extra-special touch.

1 The recycled paper used here is cheap and makes great gift-wrap. Stick real leaves onto the paper and glue several into a bunch to decorate the top of the gift.

2 Cut oak-leaf shapes out of brown paper and paint with a mixture of oranges and greens. When glued onto the wrapped box they give an interesting three-dimensional effect. Add a green raffia bow.

Spattering

Spattering is a simple decorative technique.
You need a selection of gouache or poster colors,
paper, and an old toothbrush or stenciling brush. For
these gifts brown paper has been spattered with paint,
tied with raffia and string, and decorated with real and
cut-out spattered leaves. Dried twigs and berries have
been added for final decoration.

1 Take a real leaf, draw around it and cut out of paper. Alternatively, use one of the leaf templates on pages 108 – 9. Select some fall colors and mix them to a medium consistency.

2 Dip the toothbrush into the first color and run your finger across the bristles to produce a fine spray effect. Repeat with other colors. Punch a hole and add a raffia or string tie.

CHAPTER SIX
A COUNTRY CHRISTMAS

Giving and receiving presents is an important part of the Christmas celebrations. Tartan and plaid patterns will give a traditional, rustic look to your gifts especially when you enhance them with heather, pine cones, and nuts. You can use a range of different patterned materials, from wrapping paper and paper table napkins to hessian and tartan cloth. Children love finding a stocking of presents on Christmas morning. They are simple to make – the template is on page 110 – and you can use any material you have at hand. Decorate them with buttons, beads, and ribbon.

1 Make the basic stocking in yellow fabric, with a contrasting blue plaid top and Christmas trees.

2 Use blue plaid fabric as the base and add a green top and details in red plaid fabric.

3 Make a blue-and-tartan stocking. Add a tartan pocket and bows made from plaid cloth and raffia.

You can solve the problem of wrapping bulky and awkward-shaped gifts by putting them in simple fabric bags. Bags disguise the shape of a present, such as a bottle, and look fun and interesting. A combination of tartan, plaid, and hessian fabrics will give a fresh, natural look to your gifts. Using up scraps of fabric is also an economical form of wrapping gifts. Complement the country look by fraying the edge of the fabric, tying the gifts with natural string, and adding homemade tags.

1 Fold a piece of hessian in half and sew up the sides to make a bag. Sew a strip of fabric to the top of the bag. Stitch along the top and bottom edges, and thread string through the gap between the two edges.

2 To wrap a bottle, make a narrow bag and tie the top with fabric. Make a matching tag by gluing fabric onto a cardboard tag (template page 112).

3 Decorate a hessian bag with some plaid-fabric Scotties (a template is on page 110).

4 Decorate jars, filled with homemade goodies, with strips of hessian and contrasting fabrics.

Christmas Crackers

Crackers are part of a traditional Christmas and a homemade one also makes an unusual form of gift wrapping. You can put any small gift in the middle, from novelty hats and toys to something really special.

1 Cut a piece of paper 13½ by 7 inches. Cut a piece of thin cardboard 3½ by 7 inches. Cut two pieces of thin cardboard 2¾ by 7 inches. Stick some lace along the short edges of the paper.

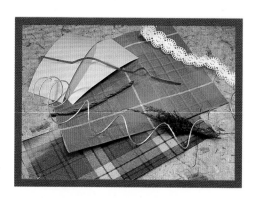

2 Roll the larger piece of cardboard into a tube and place in the middle of the paper. Put your gifts and the "snap" in the tube and fasten the paper around. Tie each end with string. Open out the ends of the paper and insert the smaller tubes.

3 Thread some paper lace onto two pieces of wire and gather it up. Tie around the "joints" of the cracker and fasten with tape. Decorate the middle and ends with ribbon and heather.

Wrap your boxes
with tartan-
patterned paper to
give an instant
festive look and add
rich, coordinating,
paper-ribbon bows.

Tie your tartan
presents with paper
ribbon, heather, and
thistles. Decorate
the lid of a wooden
box with moss,
nuts, cinnamon,
and pine cones.

Paper table napkins make cheap and fun gift wrapping. Make some simple bags by gluing the sides of a napkin together and tie the top with string and some candy. These make great going-home presents for a children's birthday party.

1 Wrap a piece of corrugated paper around several thin candles or one large candle. Add cut-out holly leaves (template page 109) and tartan-ribbon bows.

2 Tie some candles together with a tartan bow and a holly leaf made from cardboard. Make a drawstring bag from tartan fabric, fold over the top, and stitch down. Thread through a piece of string.

 A gift wrapped in fabric makes a great change from paper-wrapped gifts. Tartan fabrics are rich in both color and texture. Complement the natural look by adding bows made from cotton braids in dark, rich colors. Fresh berries, nuts, and pine cones make wonderful additional decorations. Keep an eye out for remnants of fabric, which are often sold very inexpensively. Keep all your scraps of fabric, since these can be used as ribbons or for making small bags for lavender and soap. Corn decorations bought in a store go well with these tartan gifts.

1 Cover a box with tartan fabric and tie with cotton braid. Decorate with berries, pine cones, and pine leaves.

2 Fold a rectangle of tartan fabric in half and stitch the sides together. Tie the top with string and add some corn decorations.

3 Wrap a box with fabric and decorate with nuts and pine cones. Wrap florist's wire around the base of the pine cones and push the wire into the eye of each nut. Fasten securely with glue.

CHAPTER SEVEN

ENCHANTING EASTER GIFTS

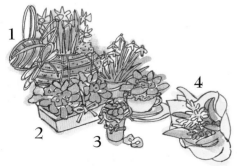

Easter, in the Western Hemisphere, coincides with the beginning of spring and the end of the cold, grey winter months. This is the time of year when the flowers burst into life and the mass of colors these produce make them wonderful Easter gifts. Keep an eye out for unusual pots and baskets for your flowers, plants, and bulbs – why not use a large china cup and saucer? Use your imagination to get more from traditional Easter eggs. Use delicate quail's eggs, paint them if you wish, as extra decoration, or fill a pretty basket with miniature foil-covered chocolate eggs. Create some original gifts by painting hen's eggs with your own designs.

1 Fill a shaped basket with potted daffodils and cover with fresh moss.

2 Fill a wooden trough or a china cup, saucer, and plate with primroses.

3 Fill small terracotta pots with snowdrops and chocolate eggs. Decorate with sugared primroses.

4 Wrap a bunch of flowers in yellow tissue paper and tie with a ribbon.

PAPERS AND TAGS

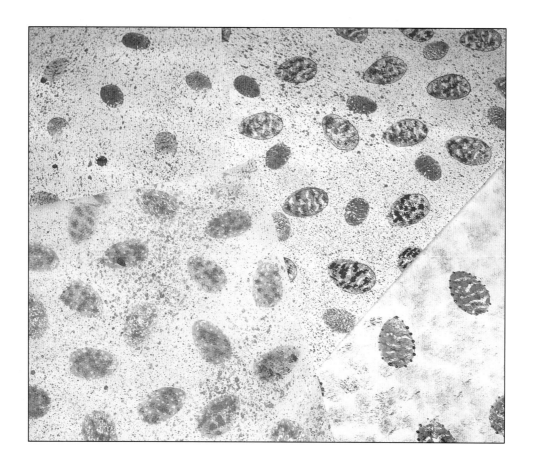

A selection of papers decorated with paint spattering and potato-print patterns (see page 76).

A mixture of bought metal tags and handmade paper ones. You will find Easter templates on page 111. Decorate with paint spattering and cutouts.

GLORIOUS GLASS

Fill glass preserve jars and pots with chocolate eggs, sweets and, nuts. Decorate with paper cutout patterns, raffia bows, and paper tags. You will find a few Easter templates on page 111.

Potato Printing

Potato printing is a simple way to decorate paper and cards. The whole family can enjoy creating a range of different effects. Buy textured paper or create an interesting base paper by first spattering paint finely over the paper. Any thickness of paper is suitable, but tissue paper looks particularly good. Choose a simple design and cut it out accurately for the best results.

1 Cut a medium-sized potato in half. Cut a stencil for your design from cardboard and then trace it onto the surface of the potato. Cut around the shape carefully with a craft knife.

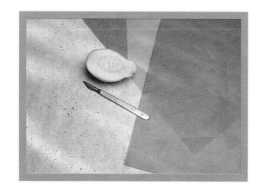

2 Mix poster colors or gouaches to a medium consistency and brush sparingly onto the potato. Press the potato evenly down onto the paper.

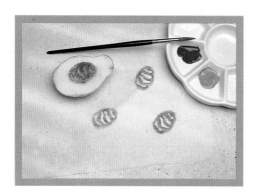

Cover boxes with spattered and potato-printed paper. Tie with silky ribbons, add some quail's eggs and a handmade tag. Fill some pretty baskets with colored, natural, and chocolate eggs.

Weaving paper is another simple technique that is great for wrapping gifts: for tags, cards, or shopping bags. Use any type of paper you have at hand – newspaper, crepe, tissue, or handmade paper. You can achieve a range of effects by weaving only parts of the paper, or by using a mixture of colors and widths of paper. The hand-painted eggs are described on page 80.

1 Fill natural and colored woven baskets with shredded tissue, straw, and a mixture of hand-painted and chocolate eggs.

2 Fold newspaper into ½ inch-wide strips. Fix a row of strips ½ inch apart and weave other strips in and out alternately to form a flat sheet. Fold the sheet in half and glue the sides to make a bag. Tape some handles to the top. Fill with raffia, eggs, and your gift.

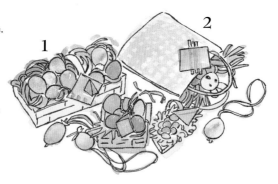

Fold a piece of paper in half to make a card. Make four narrow slits. Cut three strips of paper and decorate with egg shapes. Weave the strips in and out of the slits.

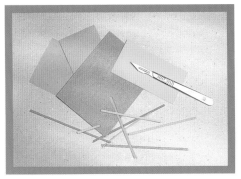

1 Cut some pretty colored paper into a tag shape. Cut several narrow strips in contrasting colors for the weaving.

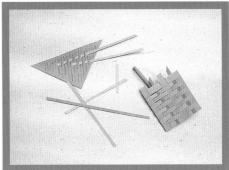

2 Cut some regularly spaced slits in the tag. Weave the first strip over and under the slits. Weave the next strip under and over. Leave the ends different lengths.

COLORED EGGS

To empty an egg, pierce it at the top and bottom with a pushpin or tack and blow the contents out gently. Rinse with water and drain on a paper towel. Paint with colored inks or thin paint. Use a needle to thread fine ribbon through the egg. Knot the end or tie on a bead.

RESIST EGGS

Paint a pattern onto your egg with masking fluid. When
it is dry, paint the egg, let it dry, and rub off the fluid.
You can also use candle wax to resist the paint.

CHAPTER EIGHT

INDIAN IDEAS

India conjures up images of vibrant-colored silks, intricate metal designs, and the wonderful colors and smells of Eastern spices. Look for specialist Indian stores that stock exquisite silks, ribbons, and accessories at reasonable prices. At Christmas you will often find unusual Indian decorations such as tassels, fabric birds, and metal ornaments. Give your gift wrapping an Eastern look by using paper and boxes in gold and rich colors with contrasting ribbons and tags.

1 Fill a marbled shopping bag with your gifts and decorate with a silk-and-metal elephant charm.

2 Tie a rust-and-gold marbled box with metallic ribbon. Decorate with gold sequins and a metal tag.

3 Tie marbled boxes with metallic and marbled ribbons. Decorate with silk and metal ornaments.

PAPERS

You can buy an amazing range of marbled paper but you can make your own version at home. Fill a large plastic trough, about $2\frac{1}{2}$ inches deep, with thin wallpaper paste. Mix two or three colors of oil paint with turpentine until they are of medium consistency. Drop spots of color onto the paste and gently stir with a knitting needle. Place your paper on the oil surface, lift it up, and leave it to dry.

TAGS

A wide selection of ornaments and tags useful for
decorating your Indian-style gifts. The brightly colored
paper labels were made of candy wrappers – see page 87.
The other ornaments were sold as Christmas decorations.
Most stores now stock a wide range of unusual items
imported from the East.

BIRDS OF PARADISE

Buy some boxes, or paint or cover some old boxes in bright colors. Tie with metallic or brightly colored silk ribbons. Add some tassels and bright fabric birds for extra decoration.

CHAPTER NINE
TASTE OF THE ORIENT

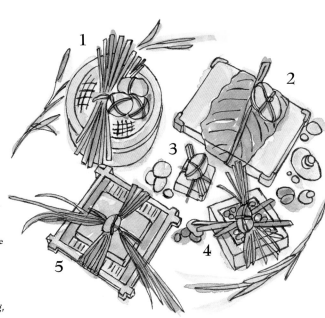

The gifts in this section take their inspiration from the colors and textures found in the Far East. These range from natural bamboo, stones, and wood to paper masks, flowers, and fans in vibrant colors. Look out for unusual Eastern-style boxes and containers that are used to present Oriental food: a bamboo steamer filled with soaps and gifts for the bathroom makes an inexpensive yet original gift.

1 Decorate a bamboo steamer with stones wired together and a bunch of grasses.

2 Wrap a wooden box with a leaf and a collection of colored stones.

3 Wrap a bar of soap in recycled paper and tie with wire, stones, and sticks of cane.

4 Fill a wooden box with decorative glass and stones. Wrap in raffia, bamboo, and grass.

5 Place your gift on a sushi board and wrap with leaves, grasses, string, and stones.

Pleated Paper

Pleating is a very versatile and simple technique. Sections of pleated paper make wonderful gift wrapping. Use fairly thin paper that can be folded easily. Vary the widths of the pleats and the width of the paper for different effects. Keep the pleating tidy and even to achieve the best results. White, textured, handmade paper looks particularly effective. The delicate pleating used on the gifts opposite captures the feel of Japanese papercraft.

1 Cut sufficient paper to wrap your box. Cut a piece of paper about twice the length of the box, for pleating. Begin folding over the width of pleat you require. Make a narrow strip of pleated paper, and a very small section for the matching tag.

2 Wrap the gift. Secure the large piece of pleated paper at one end. Gently twist the paper until the desired effect is achieved and attach the other end. Add the narrow pleated strip in the same way.

Colorful Crepe

Crepe paper in vibrant colors makes an ordinary gift look very special. Some crepe paper has a different color on the reverse side and this kind comes in handy for simple tags – made by folding a rectangle of paper in half – and for tying around gifts. Pretty paper fans make a good base for small gifts.

Festive Folding

Cover boxes with brightly colored crepe paper. Cut some strips of crepe paper, in different colors, long enough to go around the boxes. Hold the paper between your thumb and forefinger, and pull to stretch the edge of the paper slightly. Wrap these bands around the middle of the boxes. Decorate with Chinese paper flowers, fruit, and dragons.

CHAPTER TEN

NOVELTY GIFT WRAPPING

The bright and jazzy look of the gifts in this section will appeal to both children and adults. Candy is one of the main themes – it makes a great gift on its own, can be used as extra decoration, and a hard-candy shape makes a fun gift tag. Try to think up fun ways of wrapping your gifts to disguise the shape of the gift itself – the pencil on page 105 is an unusual way to wrap an odd-shaped gift. Alternatively, put your gift in a clear, plastic envelope and add some flowers and paper confetti. Wrapping ordinary boxes in colored paper and then in plain or patterned cellophane is a simple way to achieve fun gift wrapping results.

1 Paint or wrap a box in a bright primary color then wrap it in cellophane. Tie with ribbon and add a papier-mâché decoration.

2 Cover a box with patterned cellophane. Tie with shredded ribbon and a papier-mâché decoration.

3 Stick or paint numbers onto the front of a box to make it into a clock. Add hands that look like a pen and pencil. Wrap in cellophane.

4 Wrap a cone-shaped gift in cellophane. Tie with yellow raffia and a paper sunflower.

5 Wrap your gift in tissue paper and scrunch it into a ball. Cover with spotted cellophane, then tie with raffia and a decoration.

SWEET THOUGHTS

Gifts of candy and chocolate are always appreciated, especially if they are wrapped in an original way. Fill some cone-shaped cellophane bags with novelty candy shapes and tie with shredded paper and net. Small gifts wrapped in colored tissue paper in a cellophane bag also look very appealing.

STUNNING STATIONERY

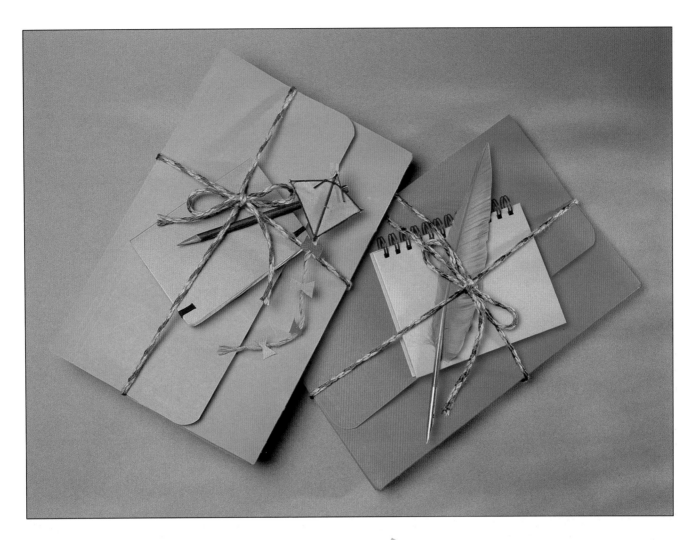

Large envelopes or folders are not expensive and make great, simple gift wrapping. Tie with string in a different color, then add a novelty pen and notebook.

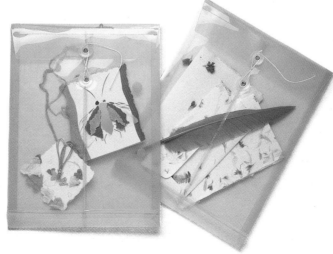

Fill transparent, colored envelopes with stationery. Add a few petals and bits of confetti for extra interest.

Fancy Dress

Make a plain box a gift in itself by decorating it to look like something else! Use your imagination to create a costume appropriate to the person receiving the gift. Utilize any of the paper techniques, such as pleating, curling, folding, and cutting, to create truly original gift wrapping.

1 Gather up a selection of colored papers and all the accessories you need. Wrap your box in plain, white paper. Start cutting strips of gray paper ¹/₂ inch wide.

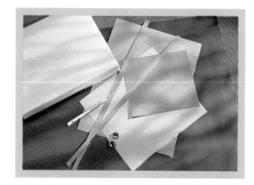

2 Wrap black paper around the box and stick it on, folding back the corners for the lapels. Attach the gray stripes, then make the flower (template page 112) and the handkerchief.

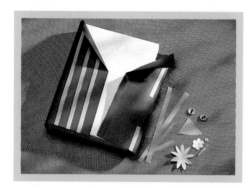

3 Cut out two bow-tie shapes (template page 112). Glue these shapes with a strip of paper. Decorate the tie and secure to the box. Cut out a label and attach the buttons.

CLASHING COLORS

Choose a paint that contrasts with the paper. Make it quite runny, dip an old toothbrush in it, and flick onto the paper. Decorate with paper ribbon and candy.

Spatter a box with a clashing paint color and make a matching tag. Wrap with paper ribbon and add some marzipan vegetables threaded onto a wooden skewer.

BOLD AND BEAUTIFUL

Decorate some brightly colored boxes with contrasting braids, clusters of sweets, or Italian biscuits wrapped in waxed papers.

Boxes in primary colors decorated with shredded paper and gift tags. Mix in some lollipops or sparklers with the paper. Gather the paper and decorations and tie at the end with some tape. Cut a small hole in the top of the box and push the bundle through.

Pencil Packaging

A large, colored-paper pencil is an unusual way to wrap a gift. Fill the pencil with novelty bits of stationery and some candy or perhaps a T-shirt, scarf, or gloves. Fill the end of the pencil with crumpled tissue paper. Make a pencil gift tag in another color.

1 Cut out a yellow rectangle 10 by 11 inches in medium-strength paper. Cut out the point of the pencil from white-and-yellow paper (see templates page 112).

2 Make the rectangle into a tube and glue down the edge. Make the yellow-and-white points into two cones, and be sure they fit inside the end of the tube. Glue the yellow cone over the white cone.

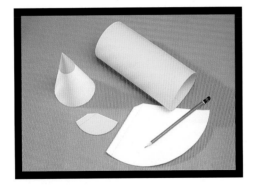

3 Make a contrasting pencil tag and thread through some plastic thread. Push the top of the pencil into the tube and secure inside with cellophane tape.

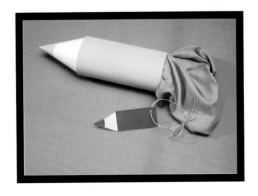

TEMPLATES

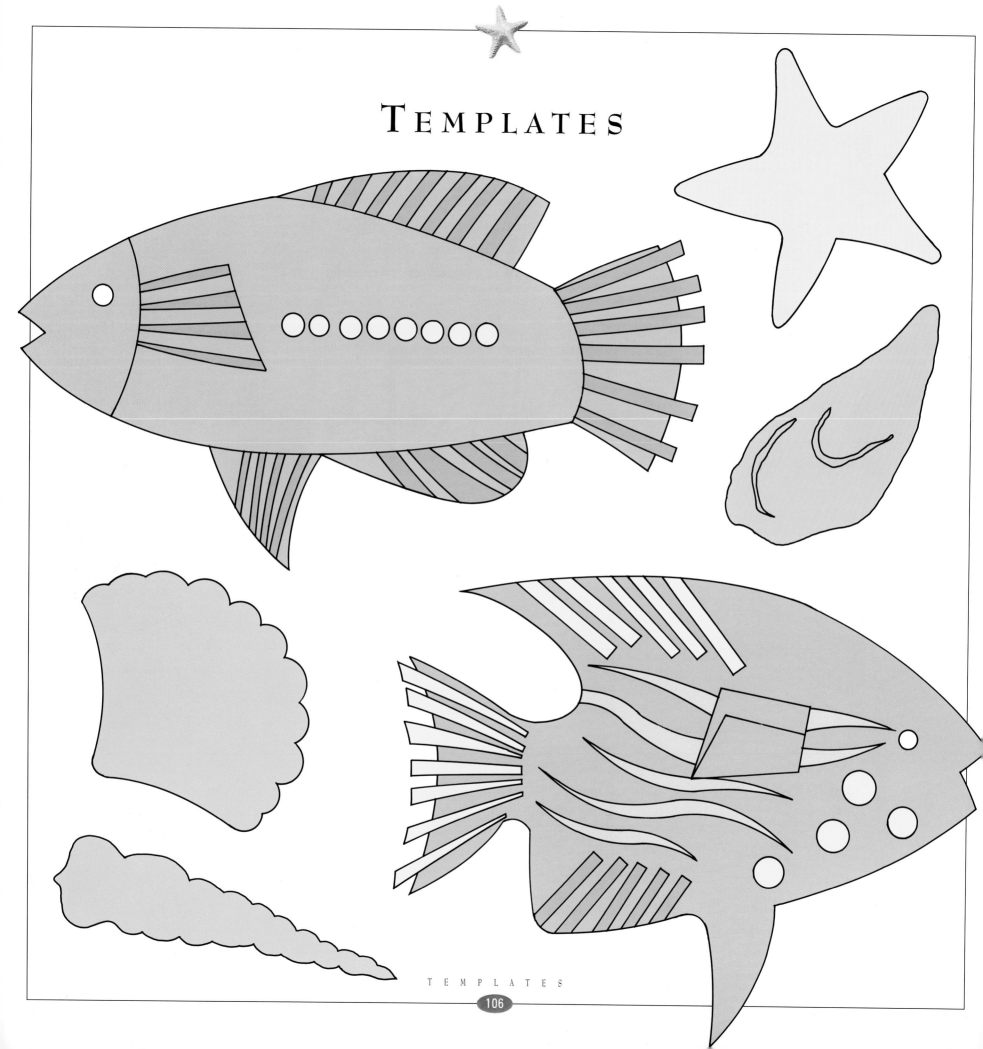

PLEASING PASTELS PAGE 35

PAPER FLOWERS PAGE 36

CUT

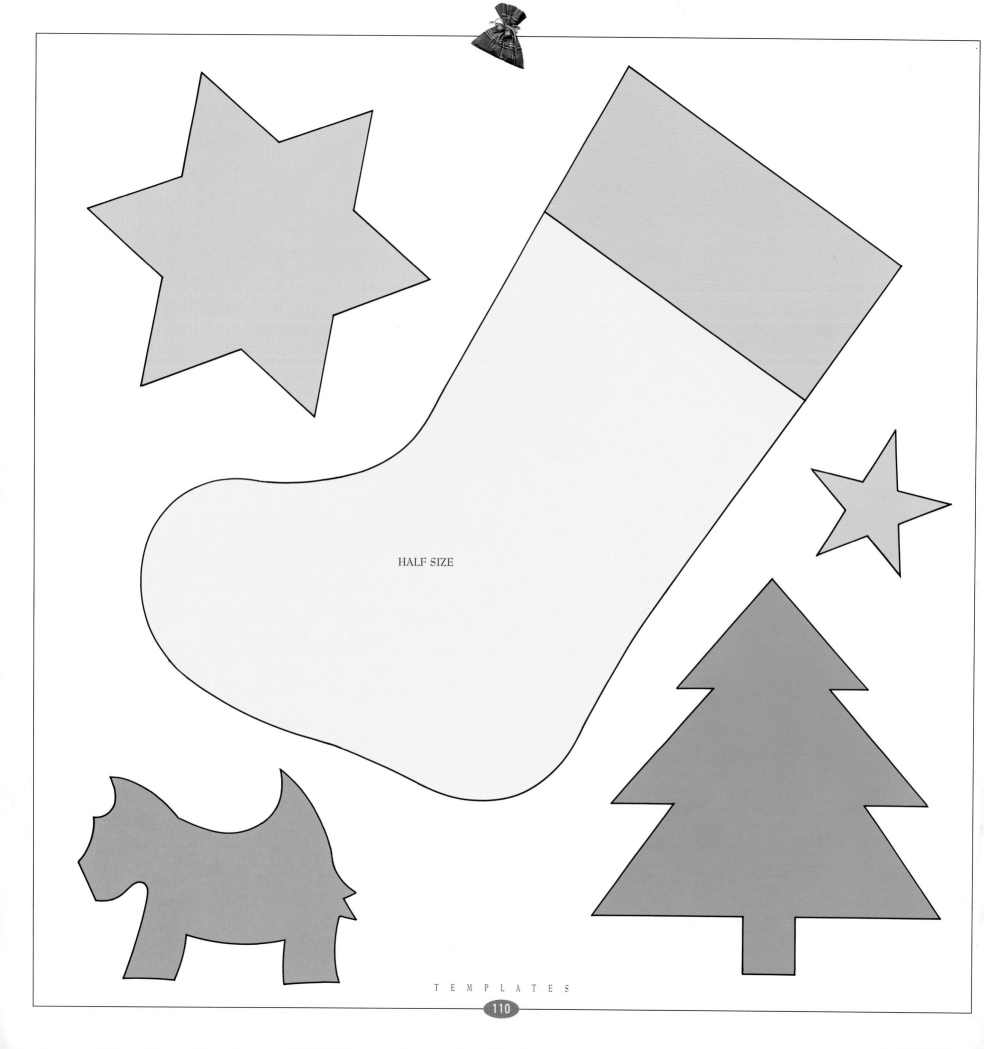

HALF SIZE

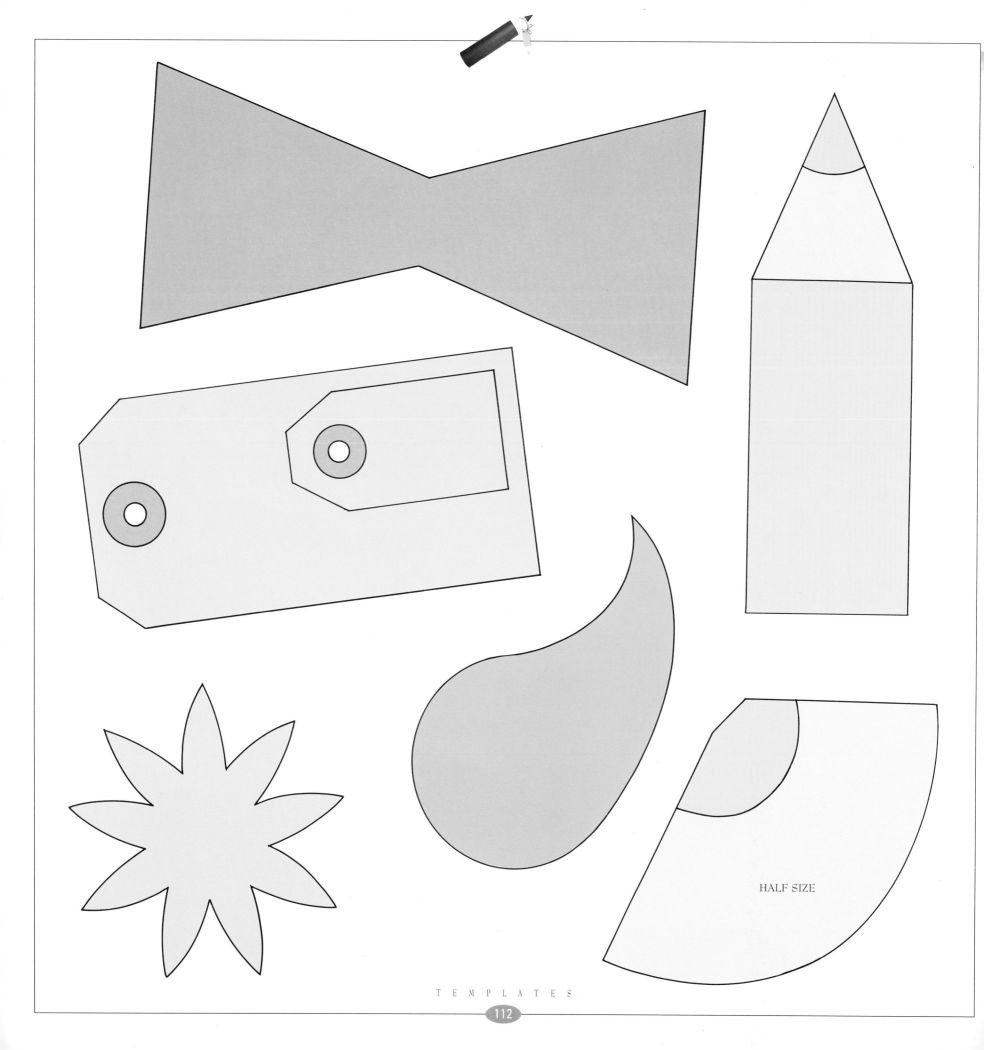

HALF SIZE

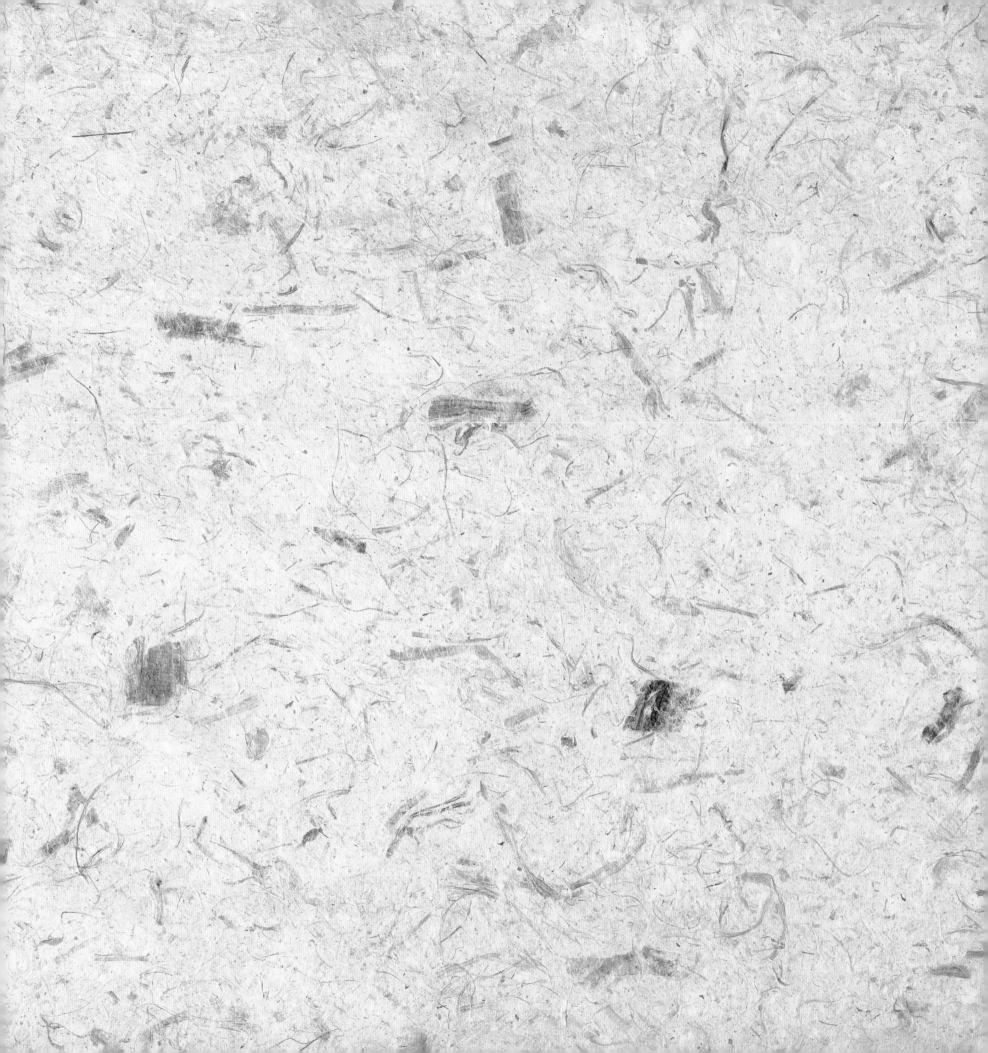